W9-BHS-974

K Y O T O
ENCOUNTERS

Shall I make a path

to visit here again?

The brilliant autumn leaves lie thick

and I cannot see the ground.

From the Kokinshū

KYOTO
ENCOUNTERS

Edited by J. Thomas Rimer

New York WEATHERHILL · *Tokyo*

© 1995 by Weatherhill, Inc. All translations by J. Thomas Rimer
except as noted. The cooperation of all photographers and publishers
who have contributed to *Kyoto Encounters* is gratefully acknowledged;
individual credits are cited in the "Notes on the Images and Authors"
and below.

First edition, 1995

Published by Weatherhill, Inc.
568 Broadway, Suite 705, New York, N.Y. 10012
Protected by copyright under the terms of the International
Copyright Union; all rights reserved.

Printed in Hong Kong

Library of Congress Cataloging in Publication Data
Kyoto encounters / edited by J. Thomas Rimer. --1st ed.
p. cm.
ISBN 0-8348-0337-2
1. Kyoto (Japan)--Pictorial works. I Rimer, J. Thomas
DS897.K843K94 1995
915.2'1864'00222--dc20   94-48166 CIP

Cover. Stone basin at Ryōanji temple (Yamashita Michitaka). *Title page.*
Stone basin at Enri-an at Sagano (Okada Katsutoshi). Anonymous
poem is from the *Kokinshū* (see note to page 55). *Page 5.* Lanterns hang
from Gion Festival floats (Yamashita Michitaka). *Page 6.* Stone lantern
amidst bellflowers at Kokushoji temple (Asano Kiichi). *Page 7.* Flower
girls in a procession at Jishu shrine (Odagaki Yoshihisa).

Contents

The heart that seeks something, I release it to the sea.

OZAKI HŌSAI

Preface

At the court of an Emperor (he lived it matters not when) there was among the many gentlewomen of the Wardrobe and Chamber one who, though she was not of very high rank, was favored far above all the rest...

SO BEGINS, IN ARTHUR WALEY'S ELEGANT TRANSLATION, the most famous of all the great monuments of Japanese literature, Lady Murasaki's *The Tale of Genji,* written in the first decades of the eleventh century. Copying the Chinese literary fashion in her generation, she purposely did not indicate the name of the city or country in which her tale takes place, but Lady Murasaki's love for Kyoto was such that within a few pages the names of specific scenes and sights in the city begin to appear. It is apparent that she, like virtually all who have come to know Kyoto before and after her, deeply loved the city.

When Lady Murasaki first wrote those lines, the capital was already over two hundred years old. Kyoto, which bore the name of Heian-kyō, or "capital of peace and tranquility," was established in 794, replacing the earlier capital of Nara, twenty miles or so to the south. The site, a flat plain surrounded by gentle hills, was appropriately selected by calling on geomancers, who divined a fortuitous location. The original city was laid out, like its predecessor, on the plan of Ch'ang An, the capital of China established by the Sui Dynasty at the end of the sixth century. In its original form, Kyoto formed a rectangle about three and a half miles long and about three miles wide. The streets and avenues were laid out in a symmetrical fashion, based on Chinese ideas of city planning, so that the city resembled a checkerboard. Later, the surrounding hills were to be filled with temples, villas, and shrines built more to Japanese taste.

As soon as the city was established as the capital and the home of the Emperor, it became a magnet for all Japan. It is clear from *The Tale of Genji,* for example, that to live in the capital was to share in the great life of the nation. When Genji was a boy, the death of his mother caused a brief exile of his family's entourage to the countryside; his servants were depressed "not so much at their mistresses' death as at being suddenly deprived of the daily sights and sensations" of the capital they loved so well. Kyoto was the seat of government, the headquarters for many of the great Buddhist sects, and soon became an important center for the ancient native Shintō religion as well. It was in Kyoto that, through the efforts of the great patrons, education, literature, music, architecture, design, painting, and calligraphy flourished. The nō theatre, which reached its highest state of development around 1400 with the troupe of Zeami, found its home and its most appreciative audiences in Kyoto. Despite the references of its name to peace and tranquility, the capital did in the course of its history suffer famines, earthquakes, civil wars, and fires. Nevertheless, there was usually, for visitors and inhabitants alike, much to learn, much to see, and so much to enjoy. In their times New York and Paris, even Berlin, have played similar roles, sometimes for hundreds of years at a stretch; Kyoto has performed that function for well over a thousand. Even though the administrative capital, and so the Emperor's residence, was shifted to Tokyo in 1868 with the Meiji Restoration heralding Japan's modern period, the powerful allure of the old capital remained.

Kyoto has long attracted visitors from abroad as well. The earliest of these travelers, in medieval times, came first from other countries of Asia, notably China and Korea. Later, when Westerners began to reach to Japan in the 1500s, important visitors included Europeans, and eventually Americans. These foreigners came for many reasons, some for trade, of course, but others for diplomacy, study, and aesthetic enjoyment. Many of these residents and visitors recorded their impressions, and the range of their responses is so vast and varied that the citations I have chosen to accompany these impressive photographs suggest a virtual history of classical, even modern Japanese literature. It is hoped that the brief "Notes on the Images and Authors" will allow those who wish to read further find translations of additional literary works that may help them to make for themselves intimate and telling connections between the physical charms of the city and its surrounding natural beauty and the poignancy and depth of the literature that those locales inspired. In this sense, Kyoto is undoubtedly the only city in Japan where the classical traditions, from those of architecture and gardening through the annual calendar of festivals, sacred and secular alike, have been maintained to an extent that permits a close and alluring congruence between, say, what a haiku poet like Matsuo Bashō saw and what he wrote. For modern readers to digest, while looking out a window in Tokyo, a haiku such as *A hermitage / Moon, chrysanthemums / And a rice field not an acre square* calls for a powerful and deliberate act of the imagination, since of all those visual elements that seized the poet's imagination, only the moon (on less polluted and smoggy nights) can be said to be readily available. Chrysanthemums are now mostly at the florist's, the hermitages have been replaced by office buildings, and the rice fields by now have been transformed into parking lots. But in Kyoto and the surrounding countryside, the exact visual details that prompted the poet's vision can, with just a little care, still be found. For Bashō's poetic response to what he has seen begins not with a cloud of vague imagination but with a sensory stimulus. In its capacity to offer such sights, from the mundane roadside flower to the grandeur of temple architecture, Kyoto surely remains unique among the cities of the world, because so much of its ancient atmosphere survives.

Kyoto, of course, does not stand still. It is the fifth largest city in Japan and an active financial and communications center. Contemporary citizens are proud of their city and its past. One example of that justifiable pride became the impetus for this present book, since these beautiful photographs were originally commissioned for an ongoing "I Love Kyoto" campaign conducted by the Bank of Kyoto, which graciously lent the plates for this present use.

All great cities offer to each visitor the chance to develop a personal, often unique relationship through the lived experience of the stranger amidst new sights, sounds, smells. And perhaps the experiences that most often leave behind for us the sharpest and most pleasurable aftertaste involve our responses not to the grandest of our prior expectations but to those small felicities that by chance engage us along our way. I hope that the juxtapositions between the photographs and texts in this book can provide glimpses of these pleasures, for most of them constitute visual and verbal records of such moments recorded in the words of those who have traveled to or been fortunate to live in "the capital of peace and tranquility" over the past millennium.

J. THOMAS RIMER

Spring

The spot

Where the spring sun sets:

Wisteria flowers.

KOBAYASHI ISSA

Mountain cherries—

Although it is the custom

To be tempted by the winds,

Wait for my visit

Before you fall.

Saigyō

I have been watching the afternoon sunlight upon the trees and the town, the shift and play of color in the crowded street of the cherry, and crooning to myself because the sky was blue and I was alive beneath it with a pair of eyes in my head.

Rudyard Kipling

Nishida often liked to walk, it is said, from the Silver Pavilion down to the small Shintō shrine at the southern end of the path. This walkway thus took on at some point the name of "Philosopher's Walk." And his strolls did not confine themselves to this trajectory. When his grandson was a primary school student, Nishida often took him along. "It was thanks to these walks," the younger Mr. Nishida said, "that I was able to visit so many spots famous in the history of Kyoto, some of them in unknown and desolate areas. Even now my memories of so many temples and shrines in Kyoto and of my grandfather himself are closely linked together. As we walked along, I would listen to the origins and traditions connected to these spots; and even though I was a child, they affected me deeply, so that I came to know something of history."

FROM A BOOK ON WALKS IN KYOTO

I hope that I may die in spring

beneath the cherry blossoms,

On the moonlight night

of the fifteenth day

Of the second month.

SAIGYŌ

Under the cherry blossoms,

None

Are altogether strangers.

Matsuo Bashō

Lingering a moment,

The moon in a night sky

Beyond the blossoms.

Matsuo Bashō

Flowers, flowers, innumerable flowers!

Flowers fade then flowers bloom again.

Flowers seem to vie with flowers:

Red flowers dazzling among brilliant white flowers!

Ishikawa Jōzan

The first rainbow:

A girl selling flowers

Goes along the Shirakawa road.

Nakagawa Shimei

Rape flowers:

The sun is in the west,

The moon is in the east.

YOSA BUSON

Once a certain man decided that it was useless for him to remain in the capital. With one or two old friends, he set out toward the east in search of a province in which to settle. Since none of the party knew the way, they blundered ahead as best they could, until in time they arrived at a place called Eight Bridges [Yatsuhashi] in Mikawa Province. Dismounting to sit under a tree near this marshy area, they ate a meal of parched rice. Someone glanced at the clumps of irises that were blooming luxuriantly in the swamp. "Compose a poem on the subject 'A Traveler's Sentiments,' beginning each line with a syllable from the word 'iris' [*kakitsubata*]," he said. The man recited:

> I have a beloved wife,
> Familiar as the skirt
> Of a well-worn robe,
> And so this distant journeying
> Fills my heart with grief.

FROM TALES OF ISE

Long after my departure,

In the old village

The cherries went on blooming.

KOBAYASHI ISSA

Spring had already passed, summer had begun, and the festival of the Kamo Shrine was already over when the Cloistered Emperor finally set out by night for Ōhara. Though this was an informal trip, he was accompanied by six nobles, eight courtiers, and some palace guards. The procession took the Kurama Road. The Cloistered Emperor stopped at an ancient temple within the city, then at the ruins where the wife of the Emperor Go-Reizei had lived in retirement as a nun. There the Cloistered Emperor got down from his carriage and entered a palanquin. He followed the road that leads to the Jakkō-in. The white clouds over the distant mountains reminded him of the cherry blossoms whirling in the wind. Spring lingered in the remaining flowers upon the fresh green boughs. It was past the twentieth day of the fourth month, so the summer grass had grown tall and thick. As the procession moved through the grass, His Majesty was gripped by a sense of complete solitude. He had never seen such a desolate place.

At the western end of Ōhara stood a small temple of but simple architecture. This was Jakkō-in.

FROM THE TALE OF THE HEIKE

Lady Rokujō:

> You ask about my carriage?
>
> I remember now
>
> That scene of long ago—
>
> The Kamo Festival,
>
> The jostling carriages.
>
> No one could tell
>
> Who their owners were,
>
> But thick as dewdrops

Priest:

> The splendid ranks crowded the place.

Lady Rokujō:

> Pleasure carriages of every description,
>
> And among them of special magnificence,
>
> The Princess Aoi's.

FROM THE SHRINE IN THE FIELDS

The kyōgen makes true things funny and funny things true.

ŌKURA TORAAKI

*H*ow delightful everything is at the time of the Festival! The leaves, which still do not cover the trees too thickly, are green and fresh. In the daytime there is no mist to hide the sky, and, glancing up, one is overcome by its beauty . . .

The young girls who are to take part in the procession have had their hair washed and arranged; but they are still wearing their everyday clothes, which are sometimes a great mess, wrinkled and coming apart at the seams. How excited they are as they run about the house, impatiently awaiting the great day, and rapping out orders to the maids: "Fit the cords on my thongs," or "See that the soles of my sandals are set right." Once they have on their Festival costumes, these same young girls, instead of prancing about the rooms, become extremely demure and walk along solemnly like priests at the head of a procession. I also enjoy seeing how their mothers, aunts, and elder sisters, dressed according to their ranks, accompany the girls and help keep their costumes in order.

SEI SHŌNAGON

Until they bloom

No one waits for them:

Azalea flowers!

Ogawa Haritsu

All that is in your heart:

You must abandon it

To the willow.

MATSUO BASHŌ

Five or six branches,

Drooping down:

Willow trees!

MUKAI KYORAI

Ah, sublime!

Young leaves, green leaves

In the glitter of the sun.

Matsuo Bashō

Summer

Ah, the dancing!

In Kyoto,

So many women!

RENSHI

*T*he purpose of *The Tale of Genji* may be likened to the man who, loving the lotus flower, must collect and store muddy and foul water in order to plant and cultivate the flower. The impure mud of illicit love affairs described in the *Tale* is there not for the purpose of being admired but for the purpose of nurturing the flower of the awareness of the sorrow of human existence. Prince Genji's conduct is like the lotus flower, which is happy and fragrant but which has its roots in filthy muddy water. But the *Tale* does not dwell on the impurity of the water; it dwells only on those who are sympathetically kind and who are aware of the sorrow of human existence, and it holds these feelings to be the basis of the good man.

MOTOORI NORINAGA

Even waking up

His eyes are drawn to them:

Green rice fields.

KOBAYASHI ISSA

35

*T*he heaven of modern humanity is indeed shattered in the Cyclopean struggle for wealth and power. The world is groping in the shadow of egotism and vulgarity. Knowledge is bought through a bad conscience, benevolence practiced for the sake of utility. The East and West, like two dragons tossed in a sea of ferment, in vain strive to regain the Jewel of Life. We need a Nu Wa to repair the grand devastation: we await the great Avatar. Meanwhile, let us have a sip of tea. The afternoon glow is brightening the bamboos, the fountains are bubbling with delight, the soughing of the pines is heard in our kettle. Let us dream of evanescence, and linger in the beautiful foolishness of things.

Okakura Tenshin

A certain hermit once said, "There is one thing that even I, who have no worldly entanglements, would be sorry to give up: the beauty of the sky." I can understand why he should have felt that way.

YOSHIDA KENKŌ

*T*he real charm of Kyoto lived in its spacious residential districts, in gates and fences and many nooks and corners, in gardens and displays of goods—all this was truly Japanese. This resembled the incomprehensible secret of architectural proportions that could not be dissolved by numbers or rules . . . there was still a connection with the classical buildings of Kyoto in their self-reliant and simple bearing.

BRUNO TAUT

*T*hese are the streets of Kyoto—Temple, Procession, Doughcake, Wealth, Willow, and Border; and to the east of Midway Street, the jewel-like palace fence encloses the five-tasseled Imperial Carriage. Next come Karasuma, Money-changers, Muromachi, Wardrobe, New, Kettle, West Temple, Little River, Oil, Samegai, and Horikawa, the street of the moated river. The level sand of the banks of Horikawa is reflected in the white waves, frost of a summer's night: even now the day breaks faintly at Shimotachiuri, this twenty-seventh day of July, the morning of the Gion Festival . . .

The Upper Town, a busy place even on ordinary days, is noisy with visitors, here for the festival, streaming downtown. People are busy sweeping and sprinkling their gates before the morning mists rise and the crowds grow thick.

CHIKAMATSU MONZAEMON

The raftsman

On his mat

Escapes from the world.

FROM MUTAMAGAWA

*B*efore the procession of a band of young men advance, leaping and wildly dancing in circles: these young men clear the way; and it is unsafe to pass near them, for they whirl about as if moved by frenzy . . . When I first saw such a band of dancers, I could imagine myself watching some old Dionysiac revel; their furious gyrations certainly realized Greek accounts of the antique sacred frenzy. There were, indeed, no Greek heads; but the bronzed lithe figures, naked save for loincloth and sandals, and most scupturesquely muscled, might well have inspired some vase design of dancing fauns. After these god-possessed dancers—whose passage swept the streets clear, scattering the crowd to right and left—came the virgin priestesses, white-robed and veiled, riding upon a horse, and followed by several mounted priests in white garments and high black caps of ceremony. Behind them advanced the ponderous shrine, swaying above the heads of its partners like a junk in a storm. Scores of brawny arms were pushing it to the right; other scores were pushing it to the left: behind and before, also, there was furious pulling and pushing; and the roar of voices uttering invocations made it impossible to hear anything else.

LAFCADIO HEARN

*I*f man were never to fade away like the dews of Adashino, never to vanish like the smoke over Toribeyama [both places for Buddhist cremation], but lingered on forever in the world, how things would lose their power to move us! The most precious thing in life is its uncertainty. Consider living creatures—none lives so long as man. The May fly waits not for the evening, the summer cicada knows neither spring nor autumn. What a wonderful unhurried feeling it is to live even a single year in perfect serenity! If that is not enough for you, you might live a thousand years and feel it was but a single night's dream.

YOSHIDA KENKŌ

*T*hey have a festival they call Bon and it is celebrated for the souls of the departed on August fifteenth every year . . . The people walk through the streets during the whole night, some out of devotion to their dead and others out curiosity to see what is going on. On the evening of this day they go out of the city to greet the souls . . . Then many people go out into the country with torches and lights and station themselves on the highest hills, declaring that they are providing light for the souls who are going back, lest they stumble on the way, and there they take leave of them.

GASPAR VILELA, S.J.

*A*ll this pushing and pulling and swaying signifies only the deity's inspection of the dwellings on either hand. He is looking about to see whether the hearts of his worshippers are pure, and is deciding whether it will be necessary to give a warning, or to inflict a penalty. His bearers will carry him withersoever he chooses to go—through solid walls if necessary. If the shrine strikes against any house—even against an awning only—that is a sign that the god is not pleased with the dwellers in that house. If the shrine breaks part of the house, that is a serious warning. But it may happen that the god wills to enter a house—breaking his way. Then woe to the inmates, unless they flee at once through the backdoor; and the wild procession, thundering in, will wreck and rend and smash and splinter everything on the premises before the god consents to proceed upon his round.

LAFCADIO HEARN

Rain soon to fall:

Fireworks shooting up

Again and again.

OZAKI KŌYŌ

*T*hey celebrate at Miyako in the month of August the festival of Gion, for such is the name of the god in whose honor it is held. It is celebrated in the following way. First of all they portion out among the streets and craftsmen all the representations to be carried in the procession. On the morning of the day, the people form up in a sort of procession, which is led by fifteen or more triumphal carriages covered with silk and other costly trappings. These carriages, which are fitted with very high masts, carry many children who sing and play on drums and flutes. Each carriage is drawn by some thirty or forty men, and behind it proceed the craftsmen, to whom it belongs, and their badges of office. They all carry their weapons—lances, pikes, and another type of weapon which has the blade of a broad-sword fitted to the shaft of a lance. And in this way the carriages, accompanied by the craftsmen and people to whom they belong, pass by. After these there follow carriages of armed men; these vehicles are decorated with paintings of ancient events and with other very fine things, and throughout the whole morning they pass in due order in front of the temple of the idol in whose honor the festival is held.

GASPAR VILELA, S.J.

*T*he most important side industry was sericulture: mulberry trees can be grown along the borders of fields and on the poor soil of the mountainsides, and mulberry leaves form the main diet of silkworms. Despite sericulture . . . the peasants lived hard, frugal lives even compared to ordinary Japanese rice farmers. I would watch men, women, and children trudging each morning and evening through the valley on their way to and from work. Because they were too poor to own horses, and wheeled vehicles could not negotiate the steep hillsides, they walked along with their backs bent double under bamboo baskets loaded with tools, fertilizer, wood, or crops. They worked from dawn to dusk on tiny patches of land, often located miles apart. They ate a simple fare of boiled barley, buckwheat noodles, and pancakes made of wheat and millet, all garnished in the summer months by fresh vegetables and in the winter by pickled vegetables, but with almost no meat or fish . . . They lived in flimsy wooden houses, with heavy thatch roofs and sparse furnishings. In the colder months, the one cheerful spot was the sunken hearth in the center of the main room, where the family members could gather to warm themselves and talk. Since there was no chimney, the smoke from the twigs and sticks they burned filtered out through holes in the eaves. The charcoal they made was sold to more affluent are as, being too expensive for their own use. Even as late at the 1940s it was a life of grinding poverty, but the farmers quietly accepted it with dignity and self-respect, treating one another with decorum and courtesy.

Haru Reischauer

*T*agore said [in 1916] that "it is the duty of a foreigner like myself to remind Japan that she has given rise to a civilization which is perfect in its form and has evolved a sense of sight which clearly sees truth in beauty and beauty in truth. She has achieved something which is positive and complete. It is easier for a stranger to know what is in her which is truly valuable for all mankind ..." It is thus that I have been led to consider the happiness arising from the existence and discovery of beauty.

Kawabata Yasunari

*T*hose who pass—the country people on their daily routine, pilgrims on the way to a temple— pay their reverence to the statue of Jizō and often dedicate a pebble which they found nearby: the statues of Jizō are often surrounded with pebbles. According to a pious legend of the country, when dead children cross the river of Hell, the Sanzu-no-kawa, they must be robbed of all their clothing by a witch named Shōzuka no Baba, who, moreover, gives them as punishment the endless work of carrying pebbles to the edge of the river to pile up on the shore. Therefore, it is supposed that the pebbles offered by the people to the statue of Jizō are saving those children in Hell the work of having to go so far in search of the pebbles. But the most interesting popular custom with respect to the God Jizō is one I learned during one of my various trips to Nagoya. In the city of Nagoya there exists a small temple dedicated to Jizō. When certain children die, their mothers go to deposit in the temple the property of the dead, that is, tiny, lovely kimono of silk, hair ornaments, footwear, stockings, dolls, horses made of paper, tambourines, and other items as well. Soon the temple becomes filled with such relics, which are periodically destroyed in grand ritual fires, in this way being offered to Jizō, who will distribute them to the poor children who suffer in purgatory, so they will have clothing and toys with which to divert themselves.

Wenceslau de Moraes

*J*ust as important for his future use . . .
were Noguchi's visits to the famed temple gardens of Kyoto, where many treasures of painting,
sculpture, and calligraphy, now safe in museums,
were still kept. Noguchi remarked that nobody
ever went there, which was certainly true in
1931. The legendary gardens were generally
neglected, as were important architectural struc-
tures, many of which were rotting away . . . The
wild and disheveled appearance of many of the
temple gardens made a deep impression on
Noguchi, who, at the end of his life, complained
that they had been "cosmeticized." The romance
of the ruined garden, a Western idea inspired by
the East, was not foreign to him.

DORE ASHTON

A slow day:

Echoes heard

In a corner of Kyoto.

YOSA BUSON

*A*n examination of landscape gardening, as taught and practiced by the Japanese, reveals an art of considerable refinement, built upon a charming system of ethics. Following, with but rare exceptions, the model of the scenery around him, the designer is not tempted to represent nature in combinations with which he is unfamiliar. It being contrary to his principles to admit into compositions exotic productions, with the conditions and surroundings of which he is imperfectly acquainted, he invariably selected as his material the vegetation and national products of his own country.

JOSIAH CONDER

The lands of the four quarters,
  upon which you gaze out,
As far as the heavens stand as partitions,
As far as the land extends in the distance,
As far as the bluish clouds trail across the sky,
As far as the white clouds hang down
  on the horizon;

On the blue ocean
As far as the prows of ships can reach,
Without stopping to dry their oars,
On the great ocean the ships teem
  continuously;

On the roads by land
As far as the horses' hooves can
  penetrate,
The ropes of the [tribute] packages
  tightly tied,
Treading over the rocks and
  roots of trees,
They move over the long roads
  without pause, continuously;

The narrow land is made wide,
The steep land is made level.

FROM AN ANCIENT PRAYER TO THE SUN GODDESS

Form, color, name, design—

Even these are things of this floating world

And should be abandoned.

RYŌKAN

*I*t is true, of course, that Japanese garden design has nowadays become world-famous for its imitations of nature, and that experts come from all over the world to see it, but even here the view of nature tends to be intellectualized. Compared with Western "landscape gardening," of course, it can be said to be more delicate, profound, and perhaps civilized in its apprehension of nature, but the tendency nevertheless is to transmute nature into forms, and to view its separate parts without any comprehensive attempt to appreciate nature as a whole. It is the same love of detail as is seen in the miniature tree and the miniature landscape on a tray. The fondness of the Japanese for creating in one garden dozens of "scenic spots" is another witness to their failure really to appreciate the larger panoramas of nature.

HASEGAWA NYOZEKAN

It must be

As though someone

Has unstrung

These clear cascading gems.

My sleeves are too narrow

To catch them all.

ARIWARA NO NARIHIRA

Autumn

The color of dew

Is white alone;

How can it be

That it can dye

The leaves of autumn

So many shades?

FUJIWARA NO TOSHIYUKI

*I*s it because of my worldly mind that I feel lonely? On moonlight nights in autumn, when I am hopelessly sad, I often go out on the balcony and gaze dreamily at the moon. It makes me think of days gone by. People say that it is dangerous to look at the moon in solitude, but something impels me, and sitting a little withdrawn, I muse there.

LADY MURASAKI

The night hours must be advanced,
It must be the dead of night:
In the sky where the wild geese call
I see the moon traveling on.

KAKINOMOTO HITOMARO

A deep experience of anything always means a confirmation of the self. The simplest example is when people want to enjoy the flavor of food.

YAMAZAKI MASAKAZU

We are nauseated by curios. Every day new bales of rubbish come up . . . mounds of books, tons of bad bronze, holocausts of lacquer. I buy literally everything that is merely possible.

HENRY ADAMS

*T*he quality that we call beauty, however, must always grow from the realities of life, and our ancestors, forced to live in dark rooms, presently came to discover beauty in shadows, ultimately to guide shadows towards beauty's ends. . . .We do our walls in neutral colors so that the sad, fragile, dying rays can sink into absolute repose.

Tanizaki Jun'ichirō

I wonder what other joys await me in Kyoto, the widow royal city, where I will arrive tonight. Traveling is captivating hunting; you go out never guessing what bird will come along. Traveling is like wine: you drink and you can't imagine what visions will come to your mind. Surely while traveling you find all that you have within you. Without wanting to, from the innumerable impressions that overflow your eyes, you choose and select whatever corresponds more to the needs or curiosities of your soul. "Objective" truth exists only—and how insignificant it is!— in the photographic cameras and in the souls that see the world coldly, without emotion, that is, without deep contact. Those who suffer and love communicate through a mystical intercourse with the landscape they see, the people they mingle with, and the incidents they select. Therefore, every perfect traveler always creates the country where he travels.

Nikos Kazantzakis

They had walked perhaps eight miles when they saw a red glow in one of the mountain valleys, still far from where they were. They could see, too, a veil of smoke hanging over the valley and its environs. The mountain air, scented with moss, became chillier as they proceeded, and Kensaku began to wonder how it was that a nighttime festival should ever have come to be held in such a remote place. From the mountains night herons flew toward them, uttering their sharp cries. Then, as they approached Kurama, they became aware of the smell of smoke lingering in the air.

In front of every house along the street a small wood fire was burning. Each fire was surrounded on three sides by large tree roots and logs the size of a grown man. Because the street was narrow, the fires in front of the houses looked like a continuous line of flickering flames down the middle of it. They were an eerie sight, like cave fires in ancient times.

The street led into a fairly open area on one side of which was a flight of wide stone steps. On top of the steps was a great red-lacquered gate. In this open area, surrounded by the enthralled spectators, were young men carrying huge torches made of brushwood tied together with wisteria vine. They wore loincloths, leggings and straw sandals, and skimpy protective coverings on their shoulders and the backs of their hands. *"Chōsa, yōsa!"* they shouted to each other as they moved, or danced, heavily yet skillfully under the weight. Some would pretend to totter, bringing the torches dangerously close to the spectators, and some would go under the eaves of the houses, then come away before any damage was done.

SHIGA NAOYA

*T*he number of soldiers [for this procession] must be great, yet there is not one of them which has not passed Examination, and found to be thus qualified: They must be active of body, ready in the use of all sorts of Arms, and somewhat knowing in their Studies; especially well exercised and trained, which they are to a wonder: for when his Majesty moves, they go along, Horse and Foot, clothed all in black silk, and ranked before, behind, and on each side of him: They march in such comely order, that never a one is observed to go out of his place; and with such silence, that they neither speak nor make any of the least noise: Neither indeed do the Citizens move their lips when the Emperor passeth, nothing being then heard but the russling of Men and Horses.

FRANÇOIS CARON

O raftsman:

I ask you,

How hard is the wind now blowing

Upon the mountains upstream?

One autumn day in the garden of a temple in Kyoto, I had quite an extraordinary experience. The design was nothing unusual . . . But the garden's complexion had never stopped changing with every passing moment. No sooner had the afternoon sun cast bright rays on the fall colors . . . than it suddenly became veiled behind the clouds, instantaneously turning the dry garden to an ashy grey. Just a hint of the sun reemerging quickly gave way to droplets of silvery rain coming down noiselessly on the white sands, rejuvenating the moss-covered rocks with a lustrous luminescence. I was gazing at one garden and more than one garden. Expressions of joy and sadness, gaiety and grief flashed one after the other across the landscape, each changing moment exquisitely harmonized into what could only be described as a restrained stylistic unity transcending the garden's particular appearance at any one moment.

KATŌ SHŪICHI

Japan has taught the world the beauty of clean, fine-grained natural wood and the fallacy of glass and paint.

J.T. HEADLEY

There is a story of Rikyu which well illustrates the ideas of cleanliness entertained by the tea-masters. Rikyu was watching his son Sho-an as he swept and watered the garden path. "Not clean enough," said Rikyu, when Sho-an had finished his task, and bade him try again. After a weary hour the son turned to Rikyu: "Father, there is nothing more to be done. The steps have been washed for the third time, the stone lanterns and the trees are well sprinkled with water, moss and lichens are shining with a fresh verdure; not a twig, not a leaf have I left on the ground." "Young fool," chided the tea-master, "that is not the way a garden path should be swept." Saying this, Rikyu stepped into the garden, shook a tree and scattered over the garden gold and crimson leaves, scraps of the brocade of autumn! What Rikyu demanded was not cleanliness alone, but the beautiful and the natural also.

OKAKURA TENSHIN

On this road

No one comes along:

Autumn evening.

Matsuo Bashō

No one comes;

All the leaves have fallen,

And in the night,

The cries of the insects

grow weaker.

SONE NO YOSHITADA

The Golden Pavilion stands overlooking and slightly overhanging a pond in a garden which originally contained the country villa of a Kyoto nobleman in Kamakura times, and it is characteristic of Momoyama culture in that it is a work of deliberate aestheticism. It is so designed and placed as to harmonize with a landscape garden, itself the product of the most conscious, one might say literary, artifice. Indeed the structure and the garden together formed an integral whole in the minds of those who planned them, and the shape of the building was of no greater importance than the distribution of the rocks and trees...

SIR GEORGE SANSOM

He pulls up the radish,

And he points it,

To show the way.

KOBAYASHI ISSA

All together

We pick the persimmons,

We eat the persimmons.

SANTŌKA

Joy to the water:

That which sounds is the water of the waterfall.

Though the sun shines, the water rushes vigorously.

FROM THE TALE OF THE HEIKE

These golden leaves,

Reminders of autumn,

Will soon be falling

In the wintry rain.

FUJIWARA NO KANEMUNE

The blue hills of themselves

Do not move;

The white clouds of themselves

Come and go.

FROM THE FOREST OF ZEN POEMS AND SAYINGS

Winter

On fields and hills alike

Nothing moves:

A snowy morning.

CHIYO

*T*he sculpture and architecture of Japan can both be characterized by the same attempt to free themselves from space as expressed in a predominance of the use of line and in a taste for simplicity and the void... This attraction to simplicity derives from a nostalgia for the infinite as well as from an effort to remove differences in space. It is the essence which is sought after, the infinitude which lies at the base of everything. What is the meaning of "close"? of "far"? God is often closer to us than our own sense of self. The mountain in the distance often seems more immediate than the trees nearby.

KUKI SHŪZŌ

The winter wind

Finishes

In the sound of the sea.

IKENISHI GONSUI

Autumn is about to leave.

The memory of the lost earth

Goes down among the ferns dead decayed

By the meteorite dust in the garden.

Pan plays a skinny naked note,

His pointed lips

Turned to the existence of lead.

NISHIWAKI JUNZABURŌ

The winter wind

Blows down the setting sun

Into the sea.

NATSUME SŌSEKI

In the coolness

Inside the boat

The shell of a crab.

TAKARAI KIKAKU

*T*his city can only be known only by an activity of an ethnographic kind: you must orient yourself in it not by book, by address, but by walking, by sight, by habit, by experience; here every discovery is intense and fragile, it can be repeated or recovered only by memory of the trace it has left in you: to visit a place for the first time is thereby to begin to write it: the address not being written, it must establish its own writing.

ROLAND BARTHES

The ice, frozen on my sleeves

That cold night of winter

Is still unmelted;

And I weep all the night long

At those memories.

*G*radually the Golden Temple came to exist more deeply and more solidly within me. Each of its pillars, its Kato windows, its roof, the phoenix on top, floated clearly before my eyes, as though I could touch them with my hands. The minutest part of the temple was in perfect accord with the entire complex structure. It was like hearing a few notes of music and having the entire composition flow though one's mind: whichever part of the Golden Temple I might pick out, the entire building echoed within me.

MISHIMA YUKIO

Something moves and rustles,
At midnight moves and rustles
Beyond the sliding glass door
*   of my window.*
I peer out. Shading the moon,
The snow falls ceaselessly.

KITAHARA HAKUSHŪ

To a wineshop

Goes the warrior, alone

On a snowy night.

Hayano Hajin

When the snow begins to melt a little, or when only a small amount has fallen, it enters into all the cracks between the tiles, so that the roof is black in some places, pure white in others—most attractive.

SEI SHŌNAGON

*A*ll the phenomena of climate, which lead apparently with compelling logic to particular decisions and buildings by man, create a special mentality, a philosophic attitude, which surmounts sense and rules feeling. It ranges man on the same level as all other natural organisms as plants, trees, animals, mountains, woods, lakes, seas and even stones. All things have souls of equal values; the Shintō shrine, standing under high trees on lofty mountains or overlooking the ocean, is like a monument to the forces of nature or like a treasure book opened at the true page to tell of them. No idol is erected; there is nothing (except a mirror and salt) inside the small shrine in the interior of the great and holy buildings.

What Shintō expresses is really no religion; its gods are no gods. In principle it means the culture of the imagination and nothing else. Shintō binds the imagination to reality, thus making it fertile. This creates productive aesthetics, all the more productive as they are united to nature, that is, to reality.

Bruno Taut

Lodging at an old temple:

The night has ended,

The room is empty.

The bitter cold has kept me

   from dreaming;

Sitting quietly, I wait for

   the temple bell to strike.

RYŌKAN

Something straight
    growing on the ground,
Something sharp, blue,
    growing on the ground,
Piercing the frozen winter,
In morning's empty path where its
    green leaves glisten,
Shedding tears,
Shedding the tears,
Now repentance over, from above its
    shoulders,
Blurred bamboo roots spreading,
Something sharp, blue,
    growing on the ground.

HAGIWARA SAKUTARŌ

Plum blossoms here at hand:

Shall I go to the south?

Shall I go to the north?

YOSA BUSON

Tomorrow the theatre:

How wide awake I am!

FROM MUTAMAGAWA

Each day we meet

Both demons and Buddhas.

17 April, 1924. Dinner with Okada. A meeting of painters who choose the designs for summer kimono. All sorts of decorative themes: the rain, the wind, the waterfall, the sky with stars showing between the clouds, fireflies, bamboo fences, and so forth.

PAUL CLAUDEL

*A*ncient simplicity is gone. With the growth of pretense the people of today are satisfied with nothing but finery, with nothing but what is beyond their station or purse. You have only to look at the way our citizens' wives and daughters dress. They can hardly go further…Of recent years, ever since some ingenious Kyoto creatures started the fashion, every variety of splendid material has been used for men's and women's clothes, and the drapers' sample-books have blossomed in a riot of color. With the delicate Ukiyo stencil-patterns, multi-colored "Imperial" designs, and dappled motifs in wash-graded tints, man must now seek in other worlds for an exotic effect, for every device on earth has been exhausted. Paying for his wife's wardrobe, or his daughter's wedding trousseau, has lightened the pocket of many a merchant, and blighted his hopes in business.

IHARA SAIKAKU

Within life and death

Snow falls ceaselessly.

SANTŌKA

*I*n the stone garden of the Ryōanji, an emotion making us feel that we are shedding our selves overcomes us. It is thus impossible for us to gainsay the artistic loftiness of these gardens. Yet why is it that we experience a strong feeling of resistance nevertheless? Is it not directed against the magic spell which draws us away from reality and makes us lose our own selves? When we visit these gardens in a mood shaped by a positive active spirit, rooted in the realities of the present, no emotion of any kind overcomes us. It is when, liberated from this spirit, we happen to go there casually, that startling emotions crowd in upon us. I have often had these experiences.

TANGE KENZŌ

*A*nyone acquainted with the ways of our tea and flower masters must have noticed the religious veneration with which they regard flowers. They do not cull at random, but carefully select each branch or spray with an eye to the artistic composition they have in mind. They would be ashamed should they chance to cut more than were absolutely necessary. It may be remarked in this connection that they always associate the leaves, if there be any, with the flower, for their object is to present the whole beauty of plant life. In this respect, as in many others, their method differs from that pursued in Western countries. Here we are apt to see only the flower stems, as it were, without body, stuck promiscuously into a vase.

Okakura Tenshin

The spring comes,

Visitors enjoy the temple;

The flowers fall,

The monk who shuts the gate

remains.

from the Forest of Zen Poems and Sayings

One fell;

Then a second fell:

Camellias!

Masaoka Shiki

Notes on the Images and Authors

Names of individual photographers appear in parentheses following descriptions of scenes. All Japanese excerpts translated by J. Thomas Rimer, except where noted.

Page 8. Sunset over Byōbu Iwa cliffs on the Tango Peninsula (Murota Yasuo).

Ozaki Hōsai (1885–1926) was a remarkable poet. He began his career in a perfectly upper-middle-class manner, graduating from the University of Tokyo, marrying, and taking a job with an important insurance company. Problems with alcohol caused him to abandon his work, divorce his wife, and, eventually, to enter the Buddhist monastic life. He moved from one monastery to the other, finally ending his life living in a small hut on the Inland Sea. His highly personal poems are, in formal terms, striking avant-garde reworkings of traditional haiku conventions. This example is Hiroaki Satō's translation from *Right Under the Big Sky, I Don't Wear a Hat: The Haiku and Prose of Hōsai Ozaki* (Stone Bridge Press, by permission).

Spring

Page 13. Wisteria hanging in the garden of Jōnangu shrine (Murota Yasuo).

The poem is by Kobayashi Issa (1763–1827), the most noted haiku poet of his day. From a poor family, Issa lived a life of poverty and wrote with moving gentleness and simplicity of the relation between man and nature.

Page 14. Cherry trees along the cable railway to Mount Hiei (Katō Yūichirō).

The poem is one in a sequence on spring by Saigyō (1118–90), one of the most admired poets of medieval Japan. A courtier in his youth, Saigyō abandoned the life of the capital and became a wandering monk. His poems, often involving Buddhist conceptions of consciousness and reality, have been continuously admired, and a number have been incorporated as themes in celebrated nō plays. He was to serve as a poetic and spiritual model for Matsuo Bashō (see page 18).

Page 15. Weeping cherries along the river Shirakawa in the Gion district (Murota Yasuo).

The passage is from a newspaper account of a spring visit to Kyoto by British novelist Rudyard Kipling (1865–1936), who was then a reporter and fledgling writer living in India. Kipling was fascinated by his first visit to Japan in 1889, and his "Letters from Japan" are fresh and full of his sharp and shrewd responses to a rapidly changing civilization.

Page 16. "The Philosopher's Walk," a favorite path for strollers (Bank of Kyoto).

Nishida Kitarō (1870–1945) is Japan's foremost modern philosopher; his *An Inquiry into the Good*, written in 1911, combines his knowledge of both Zen and Western philosophy. Later in life Nishida lived and taught in Kyoto, and often strolled along this Philosopher's Walk, quietly thinking through the various problems he addressed in his philosophical essays.

Page 17. A sprig of cherry blossoms at Nanzenji temple (Yamashita Michitaka).

The poem is another by Saigyō on his beloved cherry blossoms. Here, Saigyō expresses the hope that he, as a monk, may die on the same day of the year that the Buddha, according to tradition, entered Nirvana.

Page 18. Hirano Shrine, famous for its cherry festival (Hashimoto Kenji).

The haiku is by one of Japan's most admired poets, Matsuo Bashō (1644–94), who raised the simple seventeen-syllable haiku to a great form of poetic art. Many of his individual poems and travel diaries represent touchstones of elegance and profundity in the Japanese literary tradition, and his work has been widely translated and admired in the West as well.

Page 19. Maruyama Park cherry blossoms bathed in evening light (Mizuno Katsuhiko).

The second haiku is is also by Matsuo Bashō, who much admired the evanescent beauty of the cherry blossoms and often made them the subject of his poems on spring.

Page 20. Tulip garden at Amino (Takahashi Zenkō).

Ishikawa Jōzan (1583–1672) was a samurai who after the Tokugawa peace of 1600 retired to Kyoto, where he built the elegant Shisendō, or "Hall of the Poetry Immortals," in the northeast corner of the city. There he wrote poetry in classical Chinese and lived the life of an erudite hermit. This translation by Jonathan Chaves is taken from *Shisendo: Hall of the Poetry Immortals* (Weatherhill, Inc.).

Page 21. A *shirakawa-me*, or flower girl, selling flowers in front of a temple in Nishijin (Yamashiro Sumio).

The haiku is by Nakagawa Shimei (1850–1917), an accomplished haiku poet in Kyoto during the Meiji period (1868–1912). Many of his poems concern the beauty of the seasons in the city and its surroundings.

Page 22. Rape flowers in front of a sake brewery in Fushimi (Yamashita Michitaka).

Yosa Buson (1716–83) was generally considered the greatest haiku poet of the Tokugawa period (1600–1867) after Matsuo Bashō. Buson spent much of his time in Kyoto, where he was widely appreciated as a painter as well. His drawings for Bashō's great travel journal *The Narrow Road to the Deep North* (Oku no Hosomichi) are of special charm and power.

Page 23. Irises in the garden of Heian Shrine (Kobayashi Bunji).

The "certain man" is presumed to be the great poet and lover of the Heian period, Ariwara no Narihira (825–80). Many legends concerning him, as well as his poetry, are collected in one of the early classics of Japanese literature, *Tales of Ise*, compiled in the tenth century. This excerpt is from Section 9 of *Tales of Ise*, translated by Helen McCullough (Stanford University Press, by permission).

Page 24. Cherries over the thatched roofed of Shōji-ji, popularly known as the "Flower Temple" (Kobayashi Bunji).

The haiku is another by Issa (see page 13) offering a felicitous glimpse of the beauties of nature.

Page 25. Farmhouse in Ōhara engulfed in azaleas (Yamashita Michitaka).

This excerpt is translated by Hiroshi Kitagawa and Bruce T. Tsuchida from the epilogue of the fourteenth-century *The Tale of the Heike* (University of Tokyo Press, by permission), a moving chronicle of the devastating civil wars of 1185 that destroyed the power of the Kyoto court and heralded the rise of the military rulers. The *Heike* and Lady Murasaki's novel *The Tale of Genji* are the two great narratives that helped define the concerns of Japanese culture virtually down to this century.

The *Heike* has no known author; the texts we have were recited by roaming balladeers in the medieval period. This passage tells of a visit by the old retired Emperor to a former empress who has withdrawn from the world to the then remote village of Ōhara, now an easy ride by bus from Kyoto. As shown in the photograph, however, this village in spring, with its thatched farmhouse roof under carp banners flying to honor the boys of the family, still retains a remote and poetic atmosphere.

Page 26. An ornate ox-drawn carriage, used in the Aoi Festival (Hashimoto Kenji).

The passage is from a scene in the nō play *Nonomiya* (The Shrine in the Fields), often attributed to Zeami and translated by H. Paul Varley in Donald Keene's *Twenty Plays of the Nō Theater* (Columbia University Press, by permission). The story is adapted from early chapters in Lady Murasaki's classic Heian novel *The Tale of Genji*. Rokujō, angry at Genji's marriage to Princess Aoi, here relives her great embarrassment when her carriage, decorated for the Kamo festival, is pushed aside by Lady Aoi's retainers.

Page 27. Kyōgen comedy at Mibu temple (Bank of Kyoto).

Ōkura Toraaki (1597–1662) was a famous kyōgen actor who wrote a celebrated treatise on the aesthetics of these delightful comic plays, which, like the Mibu kyōgen shown in the photograph, date back to medieval times.

Page 28. The Aoi Festival procession marches through the forest Tadasunomori (Yamamoto Kenzō).

A charming passage from *The Pillow Book* (Columbia University Press, by permission), the Ivan Morris translation of the witty and delightful observations and reflections of Sei Shōnagon, a rival of Lady Murasaki (see page 56) at the Heian court. She describes the same Kamo Festival (sometimes known as the Aoi or Hollyhock Festival) shown in the photograph. Her description, now around nine hundred years old, captures some of the grace and excitement still felt by the citizens of Kyoto and the city's visitors at the beauty of this annual spring occurrence.

Page 29. Azaleas surounding the Hachijō Pond at Nagaoka Tenmangu shrine (Kobayashi Bunji).

Ogawa Haritsu (1663–1747) was a talented haiku poet, as well as a gifted artisan in lacquer and pottery.

Page 30. The temple Chōhō-ji shrouded in weeping willows (Kobayashi Bunji).

The haiku by Bashō seems to suggest that all temporal things, good and bad alike, be set aside as one seeks for enlightenment.

Mukai Kyorai (1651–1704) was an important disciple of Bashō and a fine poet himself. He helped edit important collections of haiku during Bashō's lifetime, and collected his teacher's sayings and teachings on poetry.

Page 31. New maple leaves contrasting with the red of Shin'nyo-do temple (Asano Kiichi).

Another haiku by Bashō with sacred overtones appropriate for the temple portrayed.

Summer

Page 33. Dancing at the Fukuchiyama Odori Festival (Dentsu).

Renshi (1679–1742) carried on the style of haiku writing established by Bashō, trained as he was by one of Bashō's most engaging disciples, Sugiyama Sampū (1679–1742).

Page 34. Lotus flowers on the Himuro Pond in Yamashina (Murota Yasuo).

Motoori Norinaga (1730–1801) was one of the great scholars of the Japanese classics of his period. His interest in explicating ancient Japanese texts written before the heavy influx of Chinese culture into Japan helped create in his writings a sense of Japanese nationhood. This particular excerpt is from his writings on Lady Murasaki's *The Tale of Genji*, as translated in *Sources of Japanese Tradition* (William DeBary, ed., Columbia University Press, by permission).

Page 35. Terraced rice paddies by the sea at Niizaki (Dentsu).

Issa (see page 13) knew intimately the lives of the farmers and grasped their urgent concerns.

Page 36. Picking tea in Uji Tawara (Dentsu).

Okakura Tenshin (1862–1913) was a controversial figure in the world of late nineteenth-century Japanese art and culture. An early disciple of the American Ernest Fenollosa, who had taken a great interest in Japanese traditional arts while living in Japan, Okakura helped develop new theories concerning a modernizing Japanese art and helped found the Tokyo School of Fine Arts. Toward the end of his life, he became the curator for Chinese and Japanese art at the Boston Museum. His English language writings, notably *The Book of Tea*, first published in 1908, did much to spread his ideas concerning the Japanese arts and Japan's place in the world.

Page 37. The gently sloping ridge of a tea plantation (Murota Yasuo).

Yoshida Kenkō (c.1283–c.1352) was a poet and essayist who lived as a partial recluse in Kyoto. His collection of miscellaneous jottings, translated by Donald Keene as *Essays in Idleness* (Columbia University Press, by permission) is a delightful compendium of writings on a dazzling variety of subjects. The discussion of aesthetics, of which Section 20 is quoted here, became particularly famous and helped to define Japanese attitudes concerning the essential relationship between time and beauty.

Page 38. Sprinkling water on the back streets of Nishijin (Dentsu).

Bruno Taut (1880–1938) was an architect of some importance in Germany during the interwar years. A visit to Japan in 1933 turned him, like Frank Lloyd Wright, into an advocate for the beauties of traditional Japanese architecture. He designed several buildings in Tokyo and wrote a number of books and articles on Japanese architecture. This excerpt is taken from *Houses and People of Japan*, first published in 1937 (Sanseido Press, by permission).

Page 39 (top). A Gion float squeezes through narrow streets (Mizuno Katsuhiko).

Chikamatsu Monzaemon (1653–1724) was the foremost playwright of his period, and many of his puppet plays (often performed by kabuki actors as well) remain among the great classics of the Japanese stage. This excerpt, translated by Donald Keene in *Major Plays of Chikamatsu* (Columbia University Press, by permission), is from the third act of *The Drum of the Waves of Horikawa,* which was written in 1706 and was based on a vendetta carried out in Kyoto only the year before.

Page 39 (bottom). Boating through the Hozugawa rapids (Yokoyama Kenzō).

This comic poem is taken from a collection of *senryū,* or short comic verses, compiled in the volume *Mutamagawa* by the poet Kei Kiitsu (1695–1762).

Page 40. Turning a Gion Festival float (Nakata Akira).

Although the summer festival described is not the Gion Festival, American writer Lafcadio Hearn (1850–1904) remains the best of the foreign writers to capture in words the archaic energies of these traditional floats, with their connection to the ancient gods of Japan. Hearn, born of an Irish mother and a Greek father, spent his career as a wandering journalist until, upon his arrival in Japan in 1890, he took Japanese citizenship and spent the rest of his life teaching and writing about Japan in order to introduce her culture to the West. This passage is taken from his *Japan: An Interpretation*, published the year of his death.

Page 41 (top). Candles lit for the repose of souls at Adashino Nembutsuji temple (Mizuno Katsuhiko).

Another famous passage from *Essays in Idleness* by Yoshida Kenkō (see page 37). This quotation is from Section 7.

Page 41 (bottom). Bonfire in the form of the character *dai,* meaning "great," lit on the mountainside for Buddhist Obon celebration (Dentsu).

Gaspar Vilela, S.J. (1525–1572), was born in Portugal and traveled to Goa, off the coast of India, before becoming a missionary in Japan. He worked and lived in Kyoto, where he was able to observe life in the capital at close range. In 1570, he fell ill and returned to Goa, where he died. His story is told in *They Came to Japan,* by Michael Cooper (University of California Press, by permission).

Page 42 (top). The Gion Festival at night (Mizuno Katsuhiko).

Lafcadio Hearn (see page 40) here describes the floats moving through the narrow streets of the city. The god is in charge!

Page 42 (bottom). Fireworks light up a summer night in Kameoka (Asaba Tetsuji).

Ozaki Kōyō (1867–1903) is best known as one of the most sensationally popular Japanese novelists of the late-nineteenth century; his melodramatic novel *The Gold Demon* was among the most popular books ever published in Japan. While his work as a haiku poet has been somewhat obscured, he nevertheless enjoyed during his lifetime a reputation for success in this form as well.

Page 43. Persian tapestries and other valuable textiles adorn a Gion festival float (Yoshida Noriyuki).

Another descriptive passage concerning Kyoto from the pen of Gaspar Vilela (see page 41).

Page 44. Washing dyed textiles called *yūzen* in the Kamo River (Kobayashi Bunji).

Haru Reischauer (born 1915) is the wife of Edwin O. Reischauer, formerly professor of Japanese history at Harvard University and an ambassador to Japan. Mrs. Reischauer's 1986 autobiography *Samurai and Silk* (Harvard University Press; copyright 1986 by the President and Fellows of Harvard University, by permission) presents a evocative account of her life as a member of the Matsukata family; her grandfather, Matsukata Masayoshi (1835–1924) rose from a modest position at the end of the Tokugawa period to one of great importance in an industrializing Japan.

Page 45. The brightly lit Kita Kannon float (Murota Yasuo).

Excerpt from a lecture delivered by Kawabata Yasunari at the University of Hawaii in 1989, the year after he received the Nobel Prize for Literature. Kawabata used traditional Japanese aesthetics to create experimental novels such as *Snow Country* and *The Old Capital,* his novel about Kyoto. The Indian poet Rabindranath Tagore (1861–1941) made a powerful impression on many writers and intellectuals at the time of his visit to Japan. Kawabata was too young to have met the famous Indian but recalled seeing his photograph: "I remember even now the features and appearance of this sagelike poet, with his long bushy hair, long mustache, and beard, standing tall in loose-flowing Indian garments, and with deep piercing eyes."

Page 46 Festival for children at a Jizō shrine (Mizuno Katsuhiko).

Wenceslau de Moraes (1851–1929), sometimes described as "the Portuguese Lafcadio Hearn," was for some years a naval officer; when his ship docked in Japan, he found himself so fascinated by the country that he took a job as the Portuguese consul in Kobe. Eventually he married and retired to the city of Tokushima, where he lived in retirement and increasing poverty, writing on Japanese culture until his death. The citation quoted here comes from his *Bon-Odori in Tokushima,* first published in 1916 (Union Press, Osaka, by permission).

Page 47. The checkered temple garden at Tōfukuji (Okada Katsutoshi).

The citation is from a recent biography of Isamu Noguchi by Dore Ashton, *Noguchi East and West* (Alfred Knopf, by permission). Born in 1904, the son of poet Yone Noguchi, Isamu Noguchi began his life in Los Angeles, developing a strong interest in the arts, particularly in sculpture. Visiting Japan from 1930 to 1932, he was struck by the beauty of Kyoto's gardens. The quality of his work, which ranges from expressive sculpture to stage sets (his 1955 *King Lear* for the Royal Shakespeare Company was particularly controversial), has made him one of the most important artistic figures of the century.

Page 48. Bamboo skirting along a wall in the Gion district (Yamashita Michitaka).

Another charming haiku by Yosa Buson, who lived many years in Kyoto and loved the city in all seasons.

Page 49. Maple trees in a moss garden at Gioji temple (Okada Katsutoshi).

Josiah Conder (1852–1920) came to Japan from England as a young architect in 1877, less than a decade after the country was opened to Western influences at the beginning of the Meiji period in 1868. He taught the first generation of Japanese architects, who used Western-style design and construction techniques, and he himself designed a number of the most famous Western-style buildings in Meiji Japan, including the famous Rokumeikan, where Japanese dignitaries entertained their foreign guests. Fascinated by Japanese art and architecture, Conder was perhaps the first Westerner to write in an authoritative manner on Japanese gardens, in his classic 1893 *Landscape Gardening in Japan,* later revised and republished in 1912. The present quotation is from that book's introduction.

Page 50. The rugged shoreline of Tango Matsushima (Watanabe Iwao).

These evocative lines are from an early ritual prayer, or *norito*, addressed to the sun goddess, Amaterasu. This group of texts was already considered ancient when the *Record of Ancient Matters* (Kojiki), the earliest written chronicle of Japan, was compiled about 710. Composed long before Kyoto was founded, this description of the landscape of ancient Japan finds echoes in the beauty of the unspoiled coastline even today. The excerpt is translated by Donald Philippi in *Norito* (Princeton University Press, by permission).

Page 51. Bellflowers in the rock garden of the temple Daikomyoji (Yamashita Michitaka).

Ryōkan (1757–1831) was a notable member of a long line of Buddhist hermits going back to Saigyō (see page 14). Ryōkan spent much of his life going on pilgrimages, especially to the remote northern province of Niigata, recording his impressions and feelings in both Chinese and Japanese verse. He was also a celebrated calligrapher. This poem is translated by John Stevens in his book on Ryōkan, *One Robe, One Bowl* (Weatherhill, Inc.).

Page 52. The stone-paved approach to the Ryugen-in at Daitokuji temple (Dai Nippon Printing Company).

Hasegawa Nyozekan (1875–1969) was a notable reporter and cultural critic of a highly liberal bent, who began his career writing for the Osaka *Asahi* newspaper. His book *The Japanese Character*, from which this excerpt is taken, was assembled from essays on various aspects of Japanese history and culture he composed between 1935 and 1938.

Page 53. Kotodaki waterfall in Tamba (Watanabe Iwao).

A famous early poem on waterfalls attributed to the Heian poet and lover Ariwara no Narihira (825–80) mentioned earler (see page 23). This poem appears in Section 87 of *Tales of Ise*.

Autumn

Page 55. Garden of the Sanzen-in temple in Ōhara (Kobayashi Bunji).

A poem by the courtier and poet Fujiwara no Toshiyuki (?–901?), who held various offices in the court and served five emperors. Known and admired as a poet and calligrapher, his poems were included in the important early anthology of court poetry, the *Kokinshū* (Collection of Old and New Japanese Poetry), compiled around 920. This poem is number 257 in that collection.

Page 56. Harvest moon over Mount Henshōji in Sagano (Mizuno Katsushita).

Lady Murasaki (c.970–c.1014), author of *The Tale of Genji*, the supreme text in classical Japanese literature, kept a diary that provides revealing glimpses of her own psychology and emotional responses to the complexities of the court life in which she lived. The translation of this brief extract from that longer text is found in Donald Keene's *Anthology of Japanese Literature* (copyright 1955 by Grove Press, by permission of Grove/Atlantic, Inc.).

Page 57. Harvest moon over Ōsawa pond (Yamashita Michitaka).

The short poem is by the most famous poet of the first great collection of Japanese poetry, *The Manyōshū* (Collection of Ten Thousand Leaves), compiled in the early Heian period, in the eighth century. Kakinomoto Hitomaro (?–715?) wrote verse on both private and public subjects of a quality that has sustained his reputation as the greatest of all early Japanese poets. This translation is from *The Manyōshū*, edited by Gakujitsu Shinkōkai (Columbia University Press, by permission).

Page 58. Food market at Nishiki Ichiba (Dentsu).

Yamazaki Masakazu (born 1934) is one of postwar Japan's most respected dramatists and cultural critics. His most recent work to be published in translation is his 1994 *Individualism and the Japanese: An Alternative Approach to Cultural Comparison*, from which this brief citation on food is taken (Japan Echo, by permission).

Page 59. The monthly flea market at Kitano Shrine (Murota Yasuo).

Henry Adams (1838–1918), the American intellectual historian and novelist, made a trip to Japan in 1886 with the American artist John La Farge, partially as a way to put behind him his grief over the suicide of his wife Clover. Adams, unlike the enthusiastic La Farge, was hardly prepared to fully enjoy such a cultural adventure, and his letters from the period, despite the irony they sometimes show, reveal a person still in the throes of attempting to come to terms with himself.

Page 60. The five-story Yasaka Pagoda viewed from Kōdai-ji temple (Okada Katsutoshi).

Tanizaki Jun'ichirō (1886–1965) is one of the most sophisticated, and widely translated, novelists of modern Japan. Although he began his career as a modernist, his increasing interest in traditional Japanese culture led him to write both fiction and such essays as *In Praise of Shadows*, published serially in 1933 and 1934 (Leete's Island Books, by permission), in which he tried to capture in his own terms the beauty and significance of his national heritage. The quotation is from that essay.

Page 61. The Yasaka Pagoda at Tōji temple is designated a National Treasure (Kobayashi Bunji).

Nikos Kazantzakis (1883–1957) is probably the best-known Greek author of this century in the English-speaking world. Renowned in his own country as a playwright, novelist, and poet, his works (*Zorba the Greek*, *The Greek Passion*, and *The Last Temptation of Christ*) often show a metaphysical dimension. Kazantzakis made a trip to Japan and China in 1935, and this citation is taken from his journals, published in English as *Japan, China: A*

Journal of Two Voyages to the Far East (Simon and Schuster, by permission).

Page 62. The Kurama Fire Festival (Murota Yasuo).

Shiga Naoya (1883–1971) is one of the foremost modern Japanese novelists, admired both for his style and his understanding of human relationships. His most famous novel *A Dark Night's Passing* (Kodansha International, by permission) was mostly written in the early 1920s, although its final, crucial chapters were not completed until 1937. Most events in the novel, including the fire festival described here, take place in Kyoto.

Page 63. Drum and fife corps marching in the Festival of the Ages (Kobayashi Bunji).

François Caron (1600–1673) was born to a French family in Brussels. He joined the Dutch East India Company, eventually becoming its director in Hirado, near Nagasaki, in 1639. The story of this careful observer of Japanese customs is told in Michael Cooper's *They Came to Japan* (University of California Press, by permission).

Page 64. Autumn maples along the river Hozugawa at Arashiyama (Asano Kiichi).

Fujiwara no Sukemune (dates uncertain) was a member of the prestigious Fujiwara family. The present poem was the only one of his to be included in the *Shinkokinshū* (New Collection of Old and New Japanese Poetry), compiled in 1201; to be included, however, was a signal honor.

Page 65. Maples at Manshu-in temple (Kobayashi Bunji).

Katō Shūichi (born 1919) is one of Japan's major postwar writers and intellectuals. After studying

medicine during the war, he began his career as a writer, critic, and teacher during the occupation and postwar periods. Katō's interests led him to study both the culture of Europe, France in particular, and of traditional Japan. The citation is from the Chang Chia-Ning's translation of Katō's autobiography, *Sheep's Song* (University of California Press, by permission).

Page 66. The garden of Jōshōkoji temple (Asano Kiichi).

This brief observation is taken from J.D. Headley's 1879 *Life and Travels of General Grant*, one of a number of books written to capitalize on Grant's world tour, which took him to Japan.

Page 67. Teahouse at Kōetsuji temple (Kobayashi Bunji).

Another quote from *The Book of Tea* by Okakura Tenshin (see page 36).

Page 68. Walkway leading to Kōzanji temple (Asano Kiichi).

Sone no Yoshitada (active c. 1075) was in provincial government service; he longed to return to the capital, where he could better practice his skills in writing poetry. Yoshitada's fame increased markedly after his death, and several of his poems were to be included in the *Shinkokinshū*. This poem is number 535 in that collection. Another well-known haiku of Bashō echoes the sentiments expressed in Yoshitada's poem.

Page 69. Rokuanji temple, popularly known as the Golden Pavilion (Kobayashi Bunji)

Sir George Sansom (1883–1968) was a member of the British Foreign Service from 1904 to 1947; he later taught at Columbia University. Sansom had a second career as an historian, and his books on Japanese history and culture, written in an informed and elegant style, remain classics of their kind; this quote is from his *Japan: A Short Cultural History* (Stanford University Press, by permission).

Page 70 (top). Washing *daikon* at Yodo (Asano Kiichi).

Another amusing verse by Kobayashi Issa (see page 13). *Daikon,* Japanese radishes, are white and much larger than those familiar in the West.

Page 70 (bottom). Persimmons drying at Uji Tawara (Dentsu).

Santōka (1882–1940) was perhaps the last in a long line of Buddhist recluses stretching back to Saigyō (see page 14) and before. Like Ozaki Hōsai (see page 8) he had terrible drinking problems; after a failed suicide attempt he entered a Buddhist monastery and was ordained at the late age of forty-four. He then became a mendicant monk, begging for his food and traveling throughout the country, often unsure of his food and lodging for the day. His striking poems, this one translated by John Stevens in *Mountain Tasting* (Weatherhill, Inc.), chronicle a remarkable spiritual journey.

Page 71. Autumn leaves over the river Kibunegawa (Mizuno Katsuhiko).

Nature often serves as a literary metaphor for human forces. The beauty of this poem serves to mask the disputes between two of the great rival Buddhist monasteries in medieval Kyoto: the water signifies Kōfukuji, the sun Enryakuji. From Chapter VIII, Book I of *The Tale of the Heike* (University of Tokyo Press, by permission).

Page 72. Ginkgo tree on the grounds of the Kyoto Imperial Palace (Asano Kiichi).

Fujiwara no Kanemune (1163–1242) is another of the court poets whose work found its way into the *Shinkokinshū.* This poem is number 545 in that ancient collection.

Page 73. Mist in the Hozu Gorge (Mizuno Katsuhiko).

The *Zenrinkushū* (Forest of Zen Poems and Sayings) was compiled from various sources by the monk Eichō (d.1574), who was associated with the famous Myōshin-ji temple in Kyoto.

Winter

Page 75. Arashiyama in snow (Asano Kiichi).

Chiyo (1703–75), the most famous of the Tokugawa female haiku poets, married, then lost her husband and her child. She moved back to her home in Kaga, an area on the sea north of Kyoto, where she eventually took Buddhist orders at fifty.

Page 76. Winter landscape at Ōsawa Pond (Watanabe Iwao).

No account of the arts of Kyoto would be complete without mention of Kuki Shūzō (1888–1941), the philosopher and writer on aesthetics who, along with Nishida Kitarō, is one of the major figures in Kyoto intellectual life of this century. Kuki was the son of a famous political figure, Baron Kuki Ryūichi, who, like his son, had some interest in the arts. Kuki studied in Europe with Heidegger, lived in Paris, where he knew Jean-Paul Sartre, then returned to teach in Kyoto. His famous book on Tokugawa aesthetics, *Iki no Kôzô* (which might be loosely translated as "The Structure of the Chic"), still inexplicably untranslated, is one of the great books on Japanese aesthetics. The present quotation is from a lecture given in French by Kuki in 1928.

Page 77. Pine trees along the coast (Morisawa Yasukata).

Ikenishi Gonsui (1650–1722) was an early haiku poet in the lively and down-to-earth Danrin school of haiku composition. Gonsui knew Bashō and helped publish his early verse.

Page 78. Foggy grove in Tamba (Okada Katsutoshi).

From *In an Abandoned Garden*, by Nishiwaki Junzaburō (1894–1982), the greatest of the avant-garde Japanese poets of interwar and early postwar years. This translation by Hiroaki Satō appears in *From the Country of Eight Islands* (Doubleday & Company, by permission). A brilliant linguist and poet, Junzaburō lived in Europe and knew Eliot and Pound; later he returned to introduce surrealism into Japanese literature and translated Eliot's *Four Quartets* into Japanese.

Page 79. Snow covering Ama no Hashidate (Fukuda Shoichi).

Natsume Sōseki (1867–1916), although well known as the greatest novelist of his period, was also a fine poet who wrote both haiku and Chinese verse.

Page 80. Unloading crabs at Taiza (Dentsu).

Takarai Kikaku (1661–1707) was perhaps the earliest of Bashō's followers, known for his cleverness and quick wit. He helped edit some of Bashō's collections.

Page 81. Festival for Ebisu, god of commerce and prosperity (Kobayashi Bunji).

Roland Barthes (1915–80) is widely appreciated in this country as a literary critic. Long a professor at the prestigious Collège de France in Paris, Barthes traveled briefly to Japan, and published his reactions to Japanese civilization in a 1970 volume excerpted here from Richard Howard's translation *Empire of Signs* (copyright 1992 by Farrar, Straus & Giroux, and reprinted by permission of Hill and Wang).

Page 82. Pagoda at Daikaku-ji temple through icy branches (Asano Kiichi).

A 31-syllable waka poem by the Heian-period writer referred to as "Lady Sarashina" because of her *Sarashina Diary*, the introspective and touching account she wrote of her own life that suggests her love of literature and her sense of spiritual yearning. In the diary, she writes that she had been observing the frosty winter scene, the night sky lit up by stars, while talking with her ladies-in-waiting.

Page 83 (top). The Golden Pavilion at Rokuonji temple (Kobayashi Bunji).

Mishima Yukio (1925–70) remains Japan's most famous postwar novelist, and most of his major works have been translated into English. His 1956 novel *The Temple of the Golden Pavilion*, from which this citation is taken (Alfred Knopf, by permission), is based on an actual incident: the burning of the famous building in 1950 by a crazed Buddhist acolyte. Fascinated by the story, Mishima did considerable research before writing this evocative psychological portrait of a soul in distress.

Page 83 (bottom). Fence of cedar trunks (Murota Yasuo).

Kitahara Hakushū (1885–1942) wrote poetry in both the traditional 31-syllable waka style and in modern free verse. His earlier modern-style poetry is filled with foreign words and exotic phrases; in a later work such as this one, published in a 1922 collection titled *Autumn of Contemplation*, his work shows calmness, even severity. This translation by is taken from *Kitahara Hakushū: His Life and Poetry* (copyright 1993 by Margaret Benton Fukasawa; Cornell East Asia Series number 65, by permission).

Page 84. Traditional restaurant in Sagano (Kitaoku Kōichirō).

Hayano Hajin (1677–1742), a pupil of two of Bashō's major disciples, Kikaku (see page 80) and Ransetsu, became in turn the teacher of the greatest poet of the next generation, Yosa Buson (see page 22). Hajin began, and Buson finished, an effort to restore the seriousness of haiku, which had moved closer to a simpler, comic verse after the death of Bashō.

Page 85. The Yasaka Pagoda towering above neighborhood houses (Kobayashi Bunji).

Another sharp-eyed and evocative observation by Sei Shōnagon (see page 28).

Page 86. Stone-paved approach to Kibune Shrine (Murota Yasuo).

Another quotation from Bruno Taut (see page 38).

Page 87. Pagoda at Daikaku-ji temple through icy branches (Okada Katsutoshi).

Another poem by Ryōkan, translated by John Stevens (see page 51).

Page 88. Bamboo grove in Otokuni (Okada Katsutoshi).

Hagiwara Sakutarō (1888–1942) is generally considered the first poet to successfully compose poetry in a thoroughly modern idiom. His 1917 collection *Howling at the Moon*, from which the poem "Bamboo" translated here by Hiroaki Satō is taken (Universty of Tokyo Press, by permission), used the colloquial language to striking effect. Nishiwaki Junzaburō (see page 78) was so impressed with Hagiwara's skill that he decided to write his own early surrealist verse in Japanese, rather than in English or French.

Page 89. Red plum blossoms in front of a cedar grove (Yamashita Michitaka).

Another haiku by Yosa Buson (see page 22).

Page 90. Names of popular actors displayed at the Minamiza Kabuki Theater (Yamashita Michitaka).

Another satirical verse from the collection *Mutamagawa* (see page 39, bottom).

Page 91. Exorcism ritual at Rozanji Temple (Yamashita Michitaka).

Another evocative haiku by Santōka (see page 70, bottom).

Page 92. *Nishijin* silks woven in bright colors (Yoshida Noriyuki).

Paul Claudel (1868–1955) maintains his reputation as one of the greatest poets and playwrights of modern

France. An ardent Catholic, his work often shows a strong metaphysical edge. Claudel served as Ambassador to Japan, and his journals for the years 1921–27, often laconic, reveal a number of fascinating details about his life in Japan and his responses to Japanese culture. This passage is quoted from his *Journal*, Vol. I (copyright 1968 by Éditions Gallimard, by permission).

Page 93. Hand-dyed fabric called *yūzen* (Dentsu).

Ihara Saikaku (1642–93), the great comic writer of the Tokugawa period, often described Kyoto in comic terms in his satiric stories and sketches. This present citation is taken from his *Japanese Family Storehouse*, first published in 1688 and in English translation by G.W. Sargent in 1959 (Cambridge University Press, by permission).

Page 94. Snow highlights raked stone garden at Tōfukuji temple (Hashimoto Kenji).

A haiku on snow by Santōka (see page 70, bottom).

Page 95. Snow on the stone garden at Ryōanji temple (Yamashita Michitaka).

Tange Kenzō (born 1913) is one of Japan's leading architects and has been for several decades a figure of world stature. His writings on architecture and the arts have been widely quoted. The extract here appears in an essay entitled "Creation in Present-day Architecture and the Japanese Tradition," included by Robin Boyd in a 1962 study of the architect, *Kenzo Tange* (George Braziller, by permission).

Page 96. Flower vase at the corner of a Gion teahouse (Yamashita Michitaka).

More information on the history of the tea ceremony from Okakura Tenshin's *Book of Tea* (see page 36).

Page 97. Deva gate at Jōjakkōji temple (Asano Kiichi).

Another verse from Eichō's collection of Zen sayings (see page 73).

Page 98. Fallen camellia blossoms in the garden of Manshu-in temple (Yamashita Michitaka).

A haiku by Masaoka Shiki (1867–1902), who brought about important reforms in haiku poetry that permitted it to remain an important form of expression in modern Japan. Ill throughout much of his life, he nevertheless found the energy to encourage other poets to take up a new style of haiku. He was close to Natume Sōseki (see page 78).

The "weathermark" identifies this book as a production of Weatherhill, Inc., publishers of fine books on Asia and the Pacific. Editorial supervision: Raymond Furse. Typography, book, and cover design: Liz Trovato. Production supervision: Bill Rose. Printed and bound at Dai Nippon Printing, Hong Kong. The typeface used is Perpetua.